Memories of
Inlet Common School

Memories of
Inlet Common School

Letty E. Haynes

by Letty Kirch Haynes

DJCR Publishing
Inlet, New York

Memories of Inlet Common School

By Letty Kirch Haynes
Copyright © 2013

Design by Nancy Did It

Published by
DJCR Publishing
PO Box 355, Inlet NY 13360

Printed in the United States of America
by Patterson Printing, Michigan

ISBN 978-0-615-75748-3

Dedicated

to the

Inlet Common School Children

It was the summer of 1972 when my washing machine decided to quit, opening up for me an adventure that was to change the rest of my life. I had always spent my summers in this lovely small village of Inlet where my grandfather had laid down the roots of our family on the shores of Fourth Lake, but to which I had never ventured in the winter. Being now forced to take my dirty laundry to the local laundromat, I came in repeated contact with the owner of it, who was also a member of the school board for the small local school. Having recently lost one of the four teachers employed there, he was desperate to replace her as September was upon us. As few teachers were willing to move to this remote area with harsh winters and small

Inlet Common School's first building

pay, he was persistent in his pleas for me to come here. He knew that I was a certified teacher, but at the time was living with my four children and husband in far off Massachusetts. Again fate intervened as three of my children were leaving home that fall, one to be married and two off to colleges. We had already sold our large home intending to move to a smaller place in Massachusetts. If we moved to the house that we owned in Inlet, we were confronted with the problems of living in the home that had been my grandfather's, but had suffered damage from a fire and had not been lived in year-around for many years. Whether the ancient heating system would still operate and whether my husband could be transferred to his company's nearer office in Utica were unanswered questions, but as I had always loved the Adirondacks and as I loved teaching and was presently unemployed, we finally decided to try it.

Thus it was that I entered the small building that housed the kindergarten students, to begin the unique teaching experience that would last for nearly twenty-five years. This building had been the first schoolhouse in Inlet, and had been established in 1900 or1901. Grades one through six were housed in the larger and somewhat newer building next door, and the eight kindergarteners I encountered that day were a drastic change from anything I had experienced before.

I had first taught in Freeport, Maine where there were thirty-four students in my fifth grade class, and had then gone to Westford, Massachusetts where they were experimenting with the "open classroom" concept of having about one hundred children in the same room with four teachers. Although someone must have thought this was a great idea, I thought it was bedlam.

To return to the Inlet school, the three teachers in the other building each had two classes in their rooms, and as Kindergarten was held only in the morning in those days, I taught various classes of the older children in the afternoon, relieving each teacher of one of their two classes for at least one period of the day, so I was involved with most of the children in the school. I believe there was a total enrollment of about sixty children at that time.

Our children were our total responsibility from the time they entered the door in the morning, until they stepped on the bus in the afternoon. Each teacher planned her own art class, which had the advantage of coinciding with something the children were studying at the time. I taught my own music, having acquired a piano for the room, and with that and a frequently used record player, music was very much a part of our daily curriculum. The older children were given music by the sixth grade teacher, Mrs. Bird, who was a music major in college. We took the children out for "Gym," sliding down the steep hill behind the school in winter, and playing Kickball, Dodgeball, or other games when the weather allowed. The playground equipment consisted of four swings, a couple of see-saws, a slide, and a self-propelled merry-go-round which we soon dispensed with, as it had a tendency to pinch the unwary rider wherever the joints of the seats came together.

We had our share of accidents, the most serious being a child who fell from the slide and broke her arm. One day a mischievous child threw someone's shoe down a deep hole. After all attempts to retrieve it failed, another child ran across the road to get his grandfather's fishing pole. Even this ingenious idea did not help. The shoe is still in the hole.

We occasionally had the child who could not resist sticking his tongue onto the metal swing uprights in freezing weather, usually as the result of a dare, and finding his tongue stuck tightly, required an application of hot water to free the unwary child. Of course, we had no school nurse, our health equipment consisting of a first aid kit.

The steep hill in the back of the school was perfect for sledding.

It was always fun to play on the huge snowbanks.

Later weekly cross country skiing was introduced into the curriculum in which all grades participated. We rented skis from a nearby ski shop and skied through trails winding behind the village. Although the owner of the shop, Walter Schmid, went with us for instruction and help, it necessitated the participation of the teachers as well. I think we all enjoyed this experience.

The children learned to ski at Fern Park.

Children playing on the field behind the school with Fifth Lake in the background.

Everyone brought a bag lunch which was eaten at his own desk, though chocolate or white milk was available at the school. After lunch all of the children went outdoors for recess, weather permitting, still being supervised by the teachers, but using their imagination for their entertainment. They made forts, or acted out plays as the spirit moved them.

Even restroom breaks were not always free from student surveillance, as I had one pupil who, if I left the room, would inevitably go to the closed bathroom door and shout, "Are you in there, Mrs. Haynes?"

There was no public library in Inlet in those days. The Bookmobile visited the school every two weeks to give the children access to a variety of books.

The atmosphere of the school was quite relaxed. Parents wandered in with forgotten lunches or books. Officials calling for "building superintendents" or indeed "superintendents" were surprised to find none available. One concerned distributer of annual tests called to make sure they would be locked in the safe upon arrival. When informed we had no safe, she wanted them secured in a locked drawer. In spite of these precautions, when they arrived, they were found leaning casually against the front door.

A hand-held brass school bell signaled the time for classes to begin in the morning, and summoned the students back into the school when the daily recess was over. It was a special privilege to be the bell ringer.

Although Inlet was prone to a rather transient population, some of the families had been here for more than one generation and the intimacy of our school developed a close relationship with the children through the seven years many of them spent with us. Our small classes and knowledge of family background gave teachers the opportunity to bring each child to his fullest potential. If the school lacked in some areas, academically it was ideal, with many students becoming valedictorian or salutatorian when they graduated from the Town of Webb High School to which they were transported after sixth grade. Because of our small town, it was inevitable that we knew the emotional disruptions that the children faced when families broke up, or illnesses or deaths occurred which caused such an upheaval in a child's life that it affected his ability to learn. We held many a crying child, trying to soothe a traumatic experience, in those days when such comfort was not illegal.

My building had its own bathroom and closet, and a glass enclosed entry room. Because both school buildings were built on a hill overlooking Fifth Lake, the basement areas were above ground at the rear of the buildings, thus the larger structure had a large sunny classroom next to the furnace room, but my building had only a small cave-like opening under the building. Here at one time was found a stash of "girlie" magazines which some of the older boys found very entertaining until noticed by the teachers. Soon afterward this lovely cave was sealed.

At this time there were no computers, of course, but I had a rather large sandbox in my room which caused some distress to the janitors as it sometimes made a mess on the floor. I found it a very useful teaching aid: marsh life became more realistic when we filled it with cattails, paper dragonflies and frogs, beaver houses of sticks, and other life found in a marsh. At Thanksgiving we filled it with Indian teepees, Pilgrims, turkeys, totem poles, etc. In the spring, pussywillows, paper spring birds, flowers etc. decorated its sand. At Christmastime we had a manger scene

This picture shows the back of the buildings with the sealed "cave" in white at the base of the kindergarten building.

ensconced there with no outraged cries from irate parents. We also made dioramas of the particular subject we were currently studying such as a unit on Holland when the sandbox contained oatmeal box windmills, dykes, and paper children in traditional dress. When it wasn't occupied by one of our projects, it was in constant use for building imaginative things or having toy car races. Sometimes I think children had more fun learning in those days than now when computers have replaced the sandbox.

Flying kites on the Inlet Golf Course. Note the old Inlet Golf Club building in the background.

The school received no state aid so teachers at this school were given a great deal of freedom in teaching as long as we followed a fairly standard curriculum of study. I often took the children on hikes through a nearby wooded area to where a picturesque bridge crossed a small stream. There we would gather colorful leaves in the fall, look for different kinds of birds or flowers, study the wildlife, or watch the changes the various seasons brought. I could load the children into my car to bring them to my home to bake gingerbread men when we read that story, or partake of other activities related to our curriculum. My husband sometimes took a day off from work to help us fly kites on the near-by golf course.

The whole school might take a day to climb one of the local mountains. When the trucks bringing fish to be "planted" in the various lakes came to town, we would go to where the fish were being loaded into helicopters or airplanes and follow them to the lake to see them being dumped. Sometimes the fish were emptied from buckets into the water near the public beach, causing many of the children to rush home for their fishing poles after school. At the end of each school year, we would include all families in a picnic at one of the public parks.

All holidays, of course, were the cause for extensive celebration. I will never forget my first Halloween here. As I was walking down the hill into town on

Luke Ernenwein looking at a soaring kite.

a moonlit Halloween night, a balmy wind was blowing the falling leaves into whirls. Suddenly, flying down the hill by the Catholic church came a figure with black witchy garments and a long tailed stocking ski hat streaming out behind. As it glided past me, I ascertained that it was our local ski instructor on roller-blades making this enchanting entrance to preface the annual parade of costumed children marching through town. What an appropriate and unusual sight. The accommodating bus driver would drive the children for trick-or-treating as the homes in this area were so scattered.

One of our year end picnics at Eighth Lake.

Local bus driver, Peggy Payne, made daily bus runs and special trips.

Every Halloween brought a trip by bus to one of the pumpkin farms. Of course our loyal bus driver, Peggy Payne, chauffeured these trips as well as the daily bus runs. Soft spoken though she was, she ran a trouble-free bus, cared for the school children as her own, and dealt with snowy roads and throwing up kids in her own calm way. She always seemed to enjoy these trips.

With no ethnic groups represented in our small community, we were free to decorate a real live evergreen tree at Christmas time. One of the children, whose father worked in the woods, usually provided the tree. We would also sing carols and present a Christmas play of whatever kind we wished. Lacking a stage at the school, this involved all of us trouping down to the Catholic Church's recreation hall, which was usually cold when we arrived, to practice. When the big night came, our program was presented there, with refreshments and a visit from Santa Claus bringing toys as the grand finale.

Other religious observances were introduced as well, including making dreidels, menorahs, etc. at Hanukah.

The children always enjoyed a trip to the pumpkin farm.

The children loved a fall hayride.

A trip to the Utica Zoo was always one of our annual pleasure trips.

As I have mentioned, the school was on a hill overlooking Fifth Lake. The broken-down wire fence, which in those days was all that separated the playing field from Fifth Lake, allowed the snapping turtles that lived in the lake to make their annual pilgrimage onto the sandy field to lay their eggs in late June. For a few days, children were kept within seeing distance only of this interesting event by one of nature's creatures. Perhaps fortunately for the baby turtles, school was dismissed for the summer before the eggs hatched.

The end of the first year came only too quickly with the closing ceremonies in which the whole school participated. For this important event, the church's hall again was used. My first class to graduate from kindergarten consisted of these children.

INLET PUBLIC SCHOOL
1973
KINDERGARTEN

Paula Heroux, Andy Townsend, Lisa McDougall, Becky Townsend, Charles Pierce, Tina Ohlweiler, and Julie Levi. I cannot identify the boy beside Lisa.

However, learning enough confidence to perform on stage, as each class did at the end of the year, was sometimes difficult. One small boy representing the sun walked onto the stage to be greeted by such laughter that he leaped crying from the stage into his mother's arms. Another boy was finally persuaded to stand motionless hidden by his "tree" as the only way to have him participate at all.

By this time, of course, I was totally enraptured by the school here, and did not for a moment consider leaving, though my husband was still trapped in Massachusetts. He did, however, manage to make the long trip every weekend.

Unfortunately, I seem to find no picture of the class of 1974. I believe Anthony Kalil, Daniel Levi, Noel Nestico, Jeffrey Pierce, Russ Beck, and Hans Schmid were in that class. Hans had been so eager to begin school, that the year before he was to start, he sometimes came the short distance from his home to visit me at home and inquire how long before he could become my student. I hope this enthusiasm stayed with him through the ensuing school years.

INLET PUBLIC SCHOOL
Inlet, New York
1974-1975
KINDERGARTEN

Adele Murdock and Stacy McDougal were absent from the class picture that year. Other classmates are Chris Canova and Carrie Hodel, top row, Willie Payne, Robin Masters, Brian Suba and Eddie Ohiler, bottom row.

Stacy McDougal, Eddie Ohwiler and Willie Payne busy with a project.

The teacher on my right is Mrs. Bird, who acted as head teacher. Realistically, we had no superintendent at the time, as the appointed one came only once or twice a year for a brief visit from his far away district.

The class of 1975 brought to the final performance, Robin Masters, Adele Murdock, Willie Payne, Chris Canova, Stacy McDougal, Carrie Hodel, Eddie Ohwiler, and Brian Suba, reciting the patriotic poem, "Hats Off."

In those days, the Enchanted Forest in Old Forge was not a water slide park, but a land of storybook characters. The little train took passengers to an Indian encampment in the back of the park where Indian teepees had been set up, campfires were kept burning, often with pots of delicious smelling food emanating from them, women weaving or sewing, and among other things, Chief Dennis carving totem poles while explaining a little about the Abanakee Indian culture. There was a western village in which the main attraction for the children seemed to be the old-time jail in which they delighted to be "restrained."

There were a few rides for small children, but the emphasis was on the storybook characters and their habitats, and the school children were usually treated to a day there near the end of the school year.

Chief Dennis carving an original Totem Pole in his Enchanted Forest retreat.

The children enjoyed the train ride at the Enchanted Forest back in the days before the water rides.

The class of 1976 consisted of Phil Caruso, Ardith Pierce, Jason Lee, Nancy Poulin, and Chris Delmarsh.

Ardie Pierce digs a hole for the willow tree we planted on Arbot Day by the side entrance to our room.

Chris Delmarsh helps her.

Some of the older children joined in the picture. Unfortunately, the tree did not survive.

Unfortunately, because of my failing memory and lack of identification, I may have made mistakes in the students in any particular class, and some children whom I know I had at some time, are missing entirely. I hope the interest in how the school used to be, and the pictures that I have been able to include will cause forgiveness for the errors and omissions.

The combined picture of the first and second grades taken in 1977, shows the former kindergarten students and my new class consisting of: Michelle Meneilly, Becky Hodel, Jerry Levi, and Danny Hitchcock. The first and second grade teacher in the upper right is Mrs. Kokernot.

Ginny Ernenwein, Kathy Ernenwein and Steve Poulin entered kindergarten together in the fall of 1978.

The number of students was dropping, and by 1978 we knew of only two girls who would be entering kindergarten in the fall, and these were twin sisters, Kathy and Ginny Ernenwein.

Many of the children who came through my door had little experience in being in any environment other than a home situation. Most were not exposed to preschool, nor being parted from family, so it took awhile for this adjustment. Given this fact and the reduction in class numbers, it seemed to me that a pre-school program would not only make the children more ready for kindergarten, but also provide a wider range of socialization. I approached the school board with the proposal to have pre-school two mornings a week. Although met with some reluctance, the main fear seeming to be that once started it couldn't be stopped, the feasibility of such a program eventually won out, and the pre-school program was started.

As it turned out there were three children who entered Kindergarten that fall, as a new family moved in with a kindergarten aged little boy, Steve Poulin, and the pre-school program, which has continued to the present time, was started on Tuesday and Thursday mornings.

I don't have a class picture of the next group of children under my tutelage. Here are a few pictures of them in various activities.

There are always some problems in any situation, no matter how idyllic, and this school was no exception. In those days there were several boys in the upper grades who were physically large and unruly in behavior. The schedule being what it was, I, of course, had them for classes in the afternoon. As the year progressed, one of the boys became in-

Jolene Wafner and Dianna Hitchcock enjoy the swings.

27

Mike Beck, back of Jolene Wafner, Kelly Green and Dianna Hitchcock.

Mike Beck and Russ Hazen in playhouse.

creasingly difficult to control. In desperation one day, Mrs Bird called the father of this boy to the school, hoping to see if something could be done to improve his behavior. It was lunch time so the other children were outside when he came. As we teachers stood in the front hall beginning to explain to the father what the problems were, he unexpectedly hauled off and delivered a punch to the boy that landed him flat on the floor. "What you need here is a man teacher, instead of all these women" he announced, and stalked away, leaving us in stunned silence behind. Needless to say, we never called him again, his son's behavior was not much improved, and we were all relieved when the boy took himself and his problems to the Old Forge school the following fall.

The main school building

Sometime around 1981, the fuel shortage became so acute that the school board decided to close the kindergarten building and house everyone in the larger building. I felt a very special tradition was lost. It had been so unique to have this original building for our very own, but environmental issues won, and the building was closed. As it turned out, this restructuring caused more than a change in buildings for me. By then, enrollment had again decreased, but the same number of classrooms were, of course needed.

Mrs. Kokernot who had been teaching first and second grades was retiring, so I was moved into the large, sunny basement room in the other building to take her place as that teacher.

The options for housing the kindergarten in the bigger building were those of a central basement room which was quite large, but rather dark and was not used for much of anything, or a smaller room upstairs that had been used as a kind of kitchen, office because it housed the telephone, and library or resource room. The only access to this room is through either of the adjoining classrooms. It was decided to use the downstairs room because it had an adjoining bathroom, a necessity for small children.

Though I had very much enjoyed having my own domain in the other building, and the kindergarten children, I was excited about trying something new. The disadvantage was that I would now be teaching the same children I had in pre-school and kindergarten, and would now have them for first and second grades, thus confining them to the same teacher for four years.

There were certainly some unique characteristics about this building, one of which was in the storage room off from the new kindergarten room. Being in the basement, the walls were rocks and cement covered by wallboard, but in this storage room, some of the cement walls were exposed, and one area had been opened out to form a large recess, apparently to be used as a bomb shelter during World War II, should the need arise, at least that is the story we were told.

This was my first combined first and second grade: First row, Carrie Pierce, Kelly Greene, Jolene Wafner, Dianna Hitchcock. Second row, Mike Beck, Russ Hazen, Luke Ernenwein, Heather Hand. Kelly, Mike, Russ, Luke, and Heather were in second grade at this time.

The end of that year brought the demonstration of the "Little Engine The Could." My forbearing husband painted all the cardboard cars to be used for the train.

Among other things stored in this room, was an old collapsible metal dentist's chair. Each year at one point, a dental hygienist would visit the school . After enlisting most of the staff to get the chair assembled to a fairly stable condition, she would examine each child's teeth. I remember one such hygienist who stayed much longer than the others. She spent a great deal of her time between each child, writing letters, knitting, and ordering supplies. Reams of small paper towels were delivered to the school which she stashed away in a little used cupboard. When she finally left, she also left these supplies, telling me to use any of them I wished. I could only believe she was given a commission for the amount she used, and must have been paid by the hour. My room being right off this room, I was more aware of her apparent negligence to duty than anyone else. I probably should have reported it to someone. This service was discontinued before long. The chair, which also disappeared, would probably be considered a valuable antique today.

It was also in this storage room that an electrical problem caused a fire to start one cold winter day. The alarm was rung, the children exited in good rehearsed order, and my group took refuge in my car out of the cold. The fire truck soon arrived, though it took longer than I would have expected because the volunteer firemen, all working at their own jobs, had to be summoned. I was told the truck couldn't roll until at least two men were on board. In those days the firehouse was in the center of town. Fortunately, the problem was quickly solved and we returned to our classes.

My room being a basement room, there were poles supporting the ceiling, which made a convenient center for the maypole dance the children really enjoyed performing every May 1st. Here is a picture of that same class engaged in that ritual.

However when the school board heard that I was celebrating May Day, I was called on the carpet and reprimanded. I am still not sure what evil political event they thought I was celebrating. These poles also made beautiful trees when we studied about the rain forest.

May Day celebration.

Seated, James Brownell and William (B.J.) Marleau. Standing, Claudette Martini, Carrie Pierce, Jolene Waffner, Diana (D.D.) Hitchcock, and Victoria Chambers

Having finally moved the second graders to another teacher, I had four new students the following year. The picture includes both classes.

1982 was the year that Greg Rudd decided to build an ice castle in Inlet. It boasted a spiral staircase, two slides, a balcony, pillars tower, gate door, drawbridge, moat, and even a dragon. Many of the school children assisted him in building this magnificent edifice that measured 15 by 15 feet, and was 20 feet high. After its completion, Rudd named Steve Poulin and Heather Hand to reign as king and queen of the castle.

The children helped Greg Rudd build an ice castle.

Steve Poulin and Heather Hand reigned over the ice castle.

The next class to enter first grade consisted of: standing at left, former students BJ Marleau, Claudette Martini, Vicki Chambers, new students Cory Greene, and James Best. Front Row: new students Emmett Emenwein, Pamela Martini, and former student James Brownsell.

Year after year new faces appeared, many of them written indelibly on my memory, some forgotten, but all so different in need and personality. The following year, it was Jason Chambers, Paul Chambers, Jason Levi, Brenda Brownell, Samantha Drake, and Eileen Ernenwein, who entered my class.

It was probably about this time one of the hazards of monitoring the playground was brought forcefully to my attention. I was standing by the front door of the school watching a hockey game being played in the parking lot, when the flying puck caught me in the back of the head, causing my head to split open and blood to come poring out. I don't remember how I was taken to the clinic twelve miles away, but stitches were taken before I could return to school.

1984's First Grade Class was, top row: Jason Chambers, Paul Chambers, Jason Levi. Bottom: Brenda Brownell, Samanthat Drake and Eileen Ernerwein.

In 1985 class members includ: top row: Paul Chambers, Jason Chambers, Jason Levi, Chris Franks; middle row: Eileen Ernenwien, Brenda Brownell, Pamalea Martini, Samantha Drake, Vanessa Leniensailor; bottom row: David Ernenwein and Patrick Martini.

In 1986 class members includ: top row: Chris Franks, Pat Martini, Paul Chambers and Vanessa Levinsailor in the back row, with Tim Pylman and Eric Reynolds in front.

One of these boys was always in trouble, though a very intelligent and endearing boy. One day, after a particularly trying afternoon, he approached me the next morning with these words, "Mrs. Haynes, you know how I acted yesterday?" To my affirmative reply he said to my amusement, "I regret that action." I often wonder what became of some of these children.

The 1987 graduating class picture shows Eric Reynalds, Judy Harvey, Tim Pylman, Steve Drake, and Angie Harvey in the back row with Patrick Martini, Jim Adams, April Chambers, Sara Van Slyke, and Ryan Sauer in the front.

In 1990 there was only one second grader, Lance Baumgardner, center. Charles Sauer, left, and Joey Ramsey, right, were the two first graders.

When 1990 came along, because of families moving, there was no one to attend second grade. We were also losing our present kindergarten teacher, so the school board decided that I should teach pre-school, Kindergarten and first grades that year. Of course, fate decreed that a second grader move in as school was about to start in September. Small though the classes were, it was still four grade levels to prepare for at an age when children are not very self directed. They can't be told to go read a book while the teacher works with another class. But we muddled through, albeit emphasizing one disadvantage of such a small school. Imagine being the only person in your class. There can be

Lance Baumgardner, who had the dubious honor of being the only student in second grade.

40

no class discussion, competition, or socialization with peers. Fortunately, the students in first grade were also boys.

Charlie Sauer, Crystal LaPorte, Amanda Capron, Rhiannon Hickox, Jessica Brownnell, and Joey Ramsey are pictured.

As I have said, Christmastime was always anticipated at school as well as home, and we always had a real tree, decorated with mostly hand-made ornaments, sang Christmas carols, exchanged presents, and closed with a party. Here is a picture at one of our Christmas parties.

In those days there was no barrier from where the teachers parked next to the school at the top of the hill. One memorable first day of April, one of the upper grade students came rushing into my classroom to tell me my car was rolling down the hill. Taken at first by surprise, I soon thought of the date and laughingly replied, Sure, April fool." Pretty soon another child arrived with the same message, and again, I, thinking how smart I was not to fall for their joke, replied the same way, only to have Mrs Bird breathlessly appear and say, "Didn't the children tell you? Your car is rolling down the hill." And indeed it was. The joke certainly was on me.

The next group of students included Amanda Smith, Erica Pylman, Angie Harvey, Todd Marleau, back row, Eric Reames, Lance Baumgartner, and George Brownsell, with Charles Sauer and Joey Ramsey at the bottom.

Charlie Sauer, top row, Todd Marleau, and Joe Ramsey; bottom, Amanda Capron, Crystal LaPorte, Jessica Brownsell and Rhiannon Hickox.

INLET COMMON
SCHOOL
GRADES 1-2
MRS HAYNES
1992-1993

This picture was taken at the Raquette Lake School as the photographer chose that location. Mike Drake, Ben Sauer, and Eric Brownsell in the back row, with Jessica Brownsell and Amanda Capron in front.

As you can tell by the class pictures from year to year, there was quite a temporary stay by some of our pupil's families.

Some activities we shared with the Raquette Lake School which was in operation at the time, though falling off in enrollment. Here we see a square dance being enjoyed by both schools. Reggie Chambers and Ann Phinney are the teachers on the left.

Competition is always in evidence in any classroom, as to who can spit the farthest, whose muscles are strongest etc. I don't think mothers would have been very flattered the day we were studying spiders and the children were caught up in a vigorous argument about whose house had the most cobwebs.

There were many observations that were made by the children which caused me much amusement. I am including a few, but one would have to have seen their serious, thoughtful faces to fully appreciate them.

"Patience is always a virgin."

"Mary is Mother Nature."

"Abe Lincoln is dead you know. He'll be dead all his life."

"President Lincoln and Washington are dust now, or maybe a fish or something."

"Witches are old girls walking on hatches."

"Mike has cankasaurus."

"Nancy has on leotights."

"Why is old people's skin so loose?"

And the excitement expressed by one child because the Glow-in-the-Dark picture he had taken home the day before, "glew" all night.

One child went home and asked his Mom if "shit was the 'F' word."

Watching a scary movie, one child declared they were "sterilized to death."

I am sure every teacher has certain projects that stand out as particularly successful or as failures. One of our most fun ones began because the news bulletins were filled with the story of whales that were stuck somewhere in Alaska. The ice had frozen around them so they had no access to the ocean. Men were trying to cut a path through the ice for them. Our class made a concentrated study of whales that year: different kinds, what they eat, their size, etc. We drew with chalk the size of a real one on the parking lot in front of the school, but what caused the most excitement was the fact that we decided to "adopt" one. For $15 one could be adopted. Thereafter the association would send a picture of "ours," where it was, its name, how it could be identified, and continue with information about it. We decided to raise the money by bringing in old toys or books the children could sell to the other children in the school for a small amount. The day arrived for the sale and I will never forget the excitement of the children running through the hall shouting, "We can buy our whale, we can buy our whale," when the $15 total had been reached. I hope some of them remember that day.

This is a picture of "our" whale. We learned that whales are identified by the marks on their tails.

The butterflies include: Eric Brownell, Ben Sauer, Jessica Brownnell, Amanda Capron, Crystal LaPorte and Michael Drake.

Another outstanding project involved another distressed species. The monarch butterflies were being doomed by the loss of their winter habitat, so the fall this first became a noticeable issue, the children all decided to make monarch wings out of cardboard and dress as butterflies for Halloween instead of their usual costumes. I thought we were quite a remarkable sight as we "flew" into town that day to display the result.

As we flew down the hill and into town.

One kindly gentleman who witnessed the event was so impressed he treated each child to a candy bar of their choice in a local store.

One year we taped off a section of floor as a space ship in which their was no gravity, so anyone entering that space had to hold on to everything he took with him, as well as keeping himself from "falling." One of the joys of this age group is the enthusiasm with which they greet all experiences.

Another time we curtained off an alcove in the room and covered the window with green tissue paper to create a "rain forest" into which we placed floor to ceiling paper trees and all the animals and plants native to the area that we could make from paper.

All projects were not so successful. One year I thought to combine healthy eating habits, manners, and writing invitations all into a project that would culminate in a little luncheon to which we would invite the current librarian. We studied healthy eating habits. We practiced setting a proper table and etiquette while eating. We wrote an invitation. I do not remember all that we served, which the children had great fun in helping prepare. The important items were the salad which contained the ordinary ingredients of lettuce, celery, carrots, and tomatoes, and the

On a warm spring day the children enjoyed blowing bubbles.

apples baked with cinnamon drops in them which we had for dessert. When I returned home that afternoon congratulating myself on the success of such a worthwhile endeavor, the phone rang and an irate mother berated me for about half an hour with the fact that I had poisoned her son by filling him full of silicates, a word I didn't even know. "All that celery and apple!" she shouted at me. I timidly explained that I had periodically notified all parents of our ongoing project, as I always did. In fact, I had bought the dressing for our salad from her in a store that very morning, mentioning that we needed it for our lunch, but she was not to be appeased. I seldom eat celery or apples to this day without remembering her tirade over something I had thought so worthwhile.

Carol Clark at her desk.

It had always been a problem to keep teachers at the Inlet school, primarily because our pay scale was so far below other districts. When I applied for the job, one of the conditions that was emphasized was that I be permanent. Most moved on as soon as a more lucrative opportunity presented itself. We could not join the teacher's union if we had wanted to because there were so few of us. I stayed because my husband was gainfully employed, so money was not a big object, and I loved the atmosphere of this unique school.

Mrs. Bird, who had come the same year I did, had similar feelings, and so we stayed on to see many other teachers come and go. I name a few for the record. There was Michelle DeCamp, Elaine Fowler, John Fowler, (no relation), Reggie Chambers, Sue Beck, Maureen Heroux, Winnie McCarley and Joan Payne Kearns, who taught for brief periods before moving to better paying schools.

After several years of teaching there, we acquired a special education teacher in the form of Carol Clark, who stayed on for several years and become a great help to students who fell within her care, and also to the teachers. She not only taught, but took care of the milk count, cleaned the microwave we had acquired by that time, and any other housekeeping tasks that needed doing.

Many times when our enrollment was really down, efforts were made by some to close the school as it would be cheaper to send everyone to Old Forge, and there were certainly some other advantages to the plan. My main concern about the Inlet school was the lack of socialization as I had classes in which there was only one boy or only one girl, and as I have said, one class with only one child.

Closing the school became a crisis situation the year the enrollment dropped to eighteen students. I have explained that we had no specific art or music teachers, or any real gym program, nor, of course, cafeteria. These seemed to be the main complaints, though some of the parents were more concerned about what they deemed the lack of teacher supervision, than had been an issue in the past. I felt we teachers were a closely knit group that worked amicably together to be aware of, and constantly improve our educational needs in this small school. The children proved this in showing so much success in the upper grades.

However, much energy was expended once again on the possibility of closing the school. And, once again, the old order won, so instead of sending the children to Old Forge where these amenities already existed, it was decided to hire part time gym, art, and music teachers, a part time superintendent, a special education teacher, and a lunch room attendant, more than doubling the faculty for far less students. The large empty room in the middle of the lower level, the kindergarten having been moved to the "office" room upstairs, was turned into a lunch room with sometimes two supervisors. So it stands today, still preserving a very unique schoolhouse in many ways.

I had often said that I would never retire, I enjoyed my job and the children so much. Each year was a new beginning, But the year came when I was offered incentive retirement, and when my husband figured out that I would make as much money staying home as teaching, I reluctantly decided it was time to stop.

One of my goals as a teacher had always been to instill in the children the importance of respecting all forms of life. "Life is a gift and is as precious to what might seem to us to be an insignificant creature as life is to us. That is the only life it has so it's as valuable as yours," I would tell the children. Whether any of this philosophy ever had any real impact on any of the children I doubt, in this area where hunting, fishing and trapping are a way of life. Indeed, did any of my contact with these children affect their lives in a positive way?

I used to show a movie to my classes done by puppets in which a caterpillar tries very hard to fly. In spite of the efforts of a bird, a squirrel, and other friends who try to help him, he fails. When in the natural course of events, he finally becomes wrapped in a cocoon and his friends realize he will turn into a butterfly, they begin to worry whether he will know them in this different form. Finally the squirrel says, "I don't know," but reassures them by adding, "Anyway, we'll know him, we'll know him."

Now when people ask me whether I think I ever had any impact on my students, whether they remember anything I tried to teach them, I say, "I don't know, but whether they do or not, I remember them and know that they all made a great impact on my life."

I learned so much from them. All those years, and all those wonderfully unique individuals and personalities filled my life with purpose and happy memories of this very special school.

So to all of those children I say, "Thanks for the memories."

A Brief History
of the Inlet Common School

The Town of Inlet was established in 1902 when it detached itself from the Town of Morehouse to become its own entity. Even before that, on January 4, 1901, land had been deeded to Charles O'Hara as trustee of School District 4 of the Town of Morehouse by James and Jennie Galvin for the sum of $76.13.

When exactly the school was built remains uncertain. Although the sign in front of the school today proclaims to passers-by that the school was built in 1906, it is probable that the smaller building opened before that. In fact, Carl Smith, one of the more recent custodians, says the words "ready for school 1903" are carved on a beam in the attic of the larger and more recent building. If that building was in use by then, it would seem the smaller one had to have been in use perhaps as early as the fall of 1901.

Mary Jane Delmarsh, daughter of the first Archie Delmarsh to run Rocky Point Inn, believes her mother, Laura Kirch Delmarsh, was the first teacher at the school where she worked before her marriage. The 1900 census lists Laura Kirch as "teacher" which seems to endorse the evidence that there was indeed an operating school at that time.

Other early teachers included Alice Burdick, Ann Burdick, Wilmer Hawthorne, Mrs. Raymond Norton, Mary Puffer Canfield, Bernard O'Hara, Alton O'Hara, John Rogers, George Blakeman Sr., Mildred Puffer, Madeline Wood, Herb Daiker, Viema McKean, Eleanor Buckley, Blanche Rupert, Ruth Rarick, Bertha Crowner, and Ora Kenwell.

Whatever the opening date, the school has struggled to and succeeded in maintaining its unique one-room school atmosphere in spite of drastic reductions in population and several attempts to close it.

About The Author

Letty Kirch Haynes was born and grew up in Watertown, New York. After high school, she went to the University of Rochester and graduated with a degree in Sociology. Returning to Watertown, she worked as a case worker in the children's division of the Jefferson County Welfare Department.

Letty Haynes

After a wonderful trip to Europe with two friends, she met her husband back in Watertown. His work as Claims Manager for Traveler's Insurance took them first to Westvale in Syracuse, then to Maine and finally to Massachusetts. Wherever they lived, they always managed to spend their summers in the Adirondacks. They had four children, two surprising them as twins.

While in Syracuse, Letty started taking courses necessary for a degree in elementary school teaching, which she began to do in Maine. When they moved full time to Letty's grandfather's old home on Fourth Lake, she taught in the Inlet Common School for twenty years.

After nearly fifty-two years of marriage, Letty lost her husband, but continues to be thankful for the beautiful place in the Adirondacks where she is privileged to live.

Also by Letty Haynes...

Memories of Inlet

On the Inlet, 4th Lake, Adirondack.

Letty Kirch Haynes

Published by North Country Books, Inc.
220 Lafayette Street, Utica, NY 13502
(315) 735-4877 • www.northcountrybooks.com